CELIA'S ISLAND JOURNAL

Written by **Celia Thaxter**

Adapted and illustrated by **Loretta Krupinski**

Little, Brown and Company
Boston   Toronto   London

ALSO BY LORETTA KRUPINSKI
Lost in the Fog

First Edition

Library of Congress Cataloging-in-Publication Data

Krupinski, Loretta.
    Celia's island journal / written by Celia Thaxter; adapted and illustrated by Loretta Krupinski. — 1st ed.
        p.   cm.
    Adaptation of: Among the Isles of Shoals / Celia Thaxter.
    Summary: Relates the experiences of a young girl growing up in the mid-nineteenth century on an isolated island off the coast of New England where her father keeps the lighthouse.
    ISBN 0-316-83921-3
    1. Isles of Shoals (Me. and N.H.) — Description and travel.
    2. Isles of Shoals (Me. and N.H.) — History. 3. Thaxter, Celia, 1835–1894.
    [1. Isles of Shoals (Me. and N.H.) — Description and travel. 2. Islands.]
    I. Thaxter, Celia, 1835–1894. Among the Isles of Shoals. II. Title.
F42.I8K78 1992
974.1'95 — dc20   91-26707

10 9 8 7 6 5 4 3 2 1

S C

Published simultaneously in Canada
by Little, Brown & Company (Canada) Limited

Printed in Hong Kong

Celia Thaxter

Celia Thaxter (1835–1894) was a published poet
and writer. As a child, she spent many years on
White Island, and later with her own family
living on Appledore Island in the Isles of Shoals
off the coast of New Hampshire. The flowers,
birds, and sea life Celia observed, which are
pictured in this book, are found on White Island.
Some bird species, in particular the puffin, are
no longer on the island, preferring to live on
more northern shores.

September 5, 1839

I will always remember my first sight of White Island where we lived after my family and I left the mainland. My father was to be the new lighthouse keeper. How excited I was on that first long sail to the Isles of Shoals. It was pleasant to listen to the slap of the water against the side of the boat, to look out at the endless sea, and to feel the warmth of the sunshine that made us blink like young sandpipers as we sat among our household goods.

The year was 1839 and it was sunset when we were set ashore on that lonely rock where the lighthouse looked down on us like some tall, black-capped giant.

September 5, 1839

Someone began to light the lamps in the tower. It made our landing seem more festive, as if the light was lit in honor of our arrival. We entered the little stone cottage that is now our home. How curious it seems with its low, whitewashed ceiling and deep window seats that show the great thickness of the walls made to keep out the sea. We slept that evening with the sound of water all around us for the first time.

January 17, 1841

The winters seem as long as a whole year. Sometimes to amuse ourselves we take pennies (for we have nothing to spend them on) and make round holes in the thick frost on the panes of glass by breathing on the coins until they are warm. Peeping out, we watch the boats scudding by. Sometimes we can even see the round head of a seal moving among the kelp-covered rocks.

February 3, 1841

On stormy days my brother and I often play in the long covered walk that lies between the tower and the house, and at night it is wonderful to watch the lighting of the lamps in the tower and think how far the lighthouse sends its rays. Father has promised me that when I grow older, I can light some of the lamps myself!

March 3, 1843

W*e survive many a dreary winter by keeping to our fireside and living with the plants, singing birds, books, and playthings that Mother and Father were wise enough to bring from the mainland. For in the stormy winter, no supply boats venture out to us. Father holds school at the kitchen table. He is teaching us reading and arithmetic. Most of all, I like to listen to Father recite poetry written by famous people.*

May 16, 1843

$\mathcal{B}$ut now it is spring, and our neighbors from Star Island rowed across. It is a pity they have no children for us to play with, but it was good to see someone else beside the family. The pilot boat from Portsmouth also arrived and brought us letters and newspapers that told us the news of the past months.

*W*ith the first warm days we danced like sandpipers on the edge of the foam and fashioned crude boats out of driftwood that we set adrift to float away forever. On a lonely ledge we startled a great blue heron, who flew off trailing legs and wings. Trees do not grow on the island, so the ledge was the highest we could climb. A flock of geese returning to the north became a floating ribbon dancing over our heads.

July 6, 1844

It is truly summer and every day we frolic in the sun. Today we launched fleets of purple mussel shells on the still pools that the tides have left among the rocks. These pools remind me of pieces of fallen rainbow because they hold seaweeds colored crimson, green, and violet. Rosy and lilac starfish cling to their sides. We laughed to see two hermit crabs fight over a moon shell. With the crab and limpet, the grasshopper and cricket, we are friends and neighbors.

August 12, 1844

I *never tire of watching the spiders. Their webs cover every window to the lighthouse top, and they rebuild them as fast as Father knocks them down. Even the rocks are draped with swinging webs. After a fog or heavy dew in the morning, every slender thread stirs with shining jewels trembling in the breeze.*

September 10, 1844

The days are noticeably shorter now, and soon autumn will be upon us and force me inside again. Few flowers ever grow here, but I will remember their bright colors with so much pleasure. My favorites are the blackberry blossoms of white, the blue-eyed grass, beach peas, and buttercups. Alas, no daisies, violets, or roses grow here, but the morning glories run wild, knotting and twisting about the rocks and smothering them with lush green leaves and pale pink blossoms. I often write poems about the beautiful things I see around me in my secret writing journal. Perhaps I will be a poet someday.

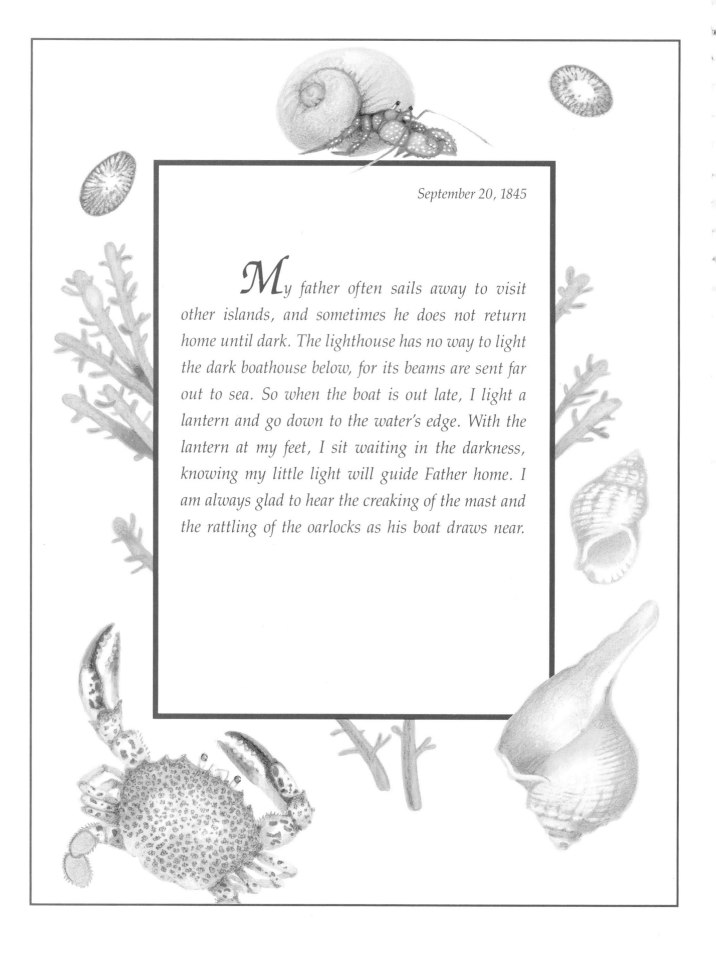

September 20, 1845

My father often sails away to visit other islands, and sometimes he does not return home until dark. The lighthouse has no way to light the dark boathouse below, for its beams are sent far out to sea. So when the boat is out late, I light a lantern and go down to the water's edge. With the lantern at my feet, I sit waiting in the darkness, knowing my little light will guide Father home. I am always glad to hear the creaking of the mast and the rattling of the oarlocks as his boat draws near.

October 17, 1845

The weather has turned much cooler, but, bundled up, we still go out to the beach to play. Today my brother and I dragged up a long seaweed from the water. Mussels were fastened to its roots. We carried those home to be cooked by Mother. Fried in crumbs or batter, they were as good as oysters. Then this afternoon I found a lobster at the edge of the rocks. I was very brave and took it in my hand, with its fierce claws attacking the air. Squealing, I ran all the way to the kitchen where Mother made it into a stew. Two treats in one day! What an adventure it is to live here.

November 1, 1846

Today was an important day. The inspector came to see if Father had been doing well in his work. The inspector was a very large man with a very large mustache and I had to caution my brother from pointing and laughing at him. We children crept into the corners, whispering and watching until the man left. My father was smiling this evening, so all must have gone well. Best of all, the inspector's boat left behind many things Father needed — wicks for the lamps, cloths to polish with, and casks of oil, all of which will be stored in the tower.

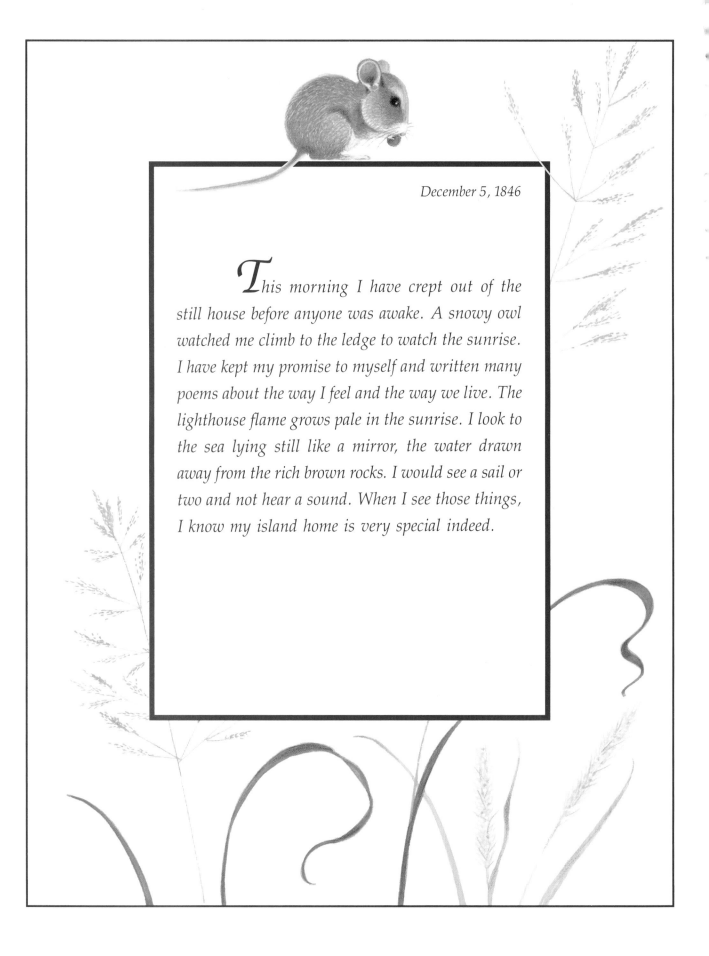

December 5, 1846

This morning I have crept out of the still house before anyone was awake. A snowy owl watched me climb to the ledge to watch the sunrise. I have kept my promise to myself and written many poems about the way I feel and the way we live. The lighthouse flame grows pale in the sunrise. I look to the sea lying still like a mirror, the water drawn away from the rich brown rocks. I would see a sail or two and not hear a sound. When I see those things, I know my island home is very special indeed.

The Sandpiper

Across the narrow beach we flit,
  One little sandpiper and I,
And fast I gather, bit by bit,
  The scattered driftwood bleached and dry.
The wild waves reach their hands for it,
  The wild wind raves, the tide runs high,
As up and down the beach we flit, —
  One little sandpiper and I.

Above our heads the sullen clouds
  Scud black and swift across the sky;
Like silent ghosts in misty shrouds
  Stand out the white lighthouses high.
Almost as far as eye can reach
  I see the close-reefed vessels fly,
As fast we flit along the beach, —
  One little sandpiper and I.

I watch him as he skims along,
  Uttering his sweet and mournful cry;
He starts not at my fitful song,
  Or flash of fluttering drapery.
He has no thought of any wrong;
  He scans me with a fearless eye:
Staunch friends are we, well tried and strong,
  The little sandpiper and I.

Celia Thaxter